CELEBRATING THE NAME KELLY

Celebrating the Name Kelly

Walter the Educator

Silent King Books

SILENT KING BOOKS

SKB

Copyright © 2024 by Walter the Educator

All rights reserved. No part of this book may be reproduced in any manner whatsoever without written permission except in the case of brief quotations embodied in critical articles and reviews.

First Printing, 2024

Disclaimer
This book is a literary work; poems are not about specific persons, locations, situations, and/or circumstances unless mentioned in a historical context. This book is for entertainment and informational purposes only. The author and publisher offer this information without warranties expressed or implied. No matter the grounds, neither the author nor the publisher will be accountable for any losses, injuries, or other damages caused by the reader's use of this book. The use of this book acknowledges an understanding and acceptance of this disclaimer.

dedicated to everyone with the first name of Kelly

KELLY

Kelly reigns supreme,

KELLY

A name that dances on the edge of a dream.

KELLY

With syllables soft, like petals in bloom,

KELLY

It carries a melody, dispelling gloom.

KELLY

In fields of emerald, where sunbeams play,

KELLY

Kelly wanders, her laughter in the sway

KELLY

Of wind-kissed grasses, that gently bend

KELLY

To touch her spirit, her essence blend.

KELLY

Her eyes, like pools of azure deep,

KELLY

Reflect the secrets that the universe keeps.

KELLY

In their depths, stars twinkle bright,

KELLY

Guiding souls through the darkest night.

KELLY

Kelly, a warrior, fearless and bold,

KELLY

With a heart of fire, yet tender to hold.

KELLY

She faces challenges with grace and might,

KELLY

Embracing the journey, bathed in light.

KELLY

In the tapestry of life, Kelly weaves

KELLY

Threads of compassion, hope she conceives.

KELLY

Each word she speaks, a healing balm,

KELLY

Calming storms with her soothing psalm.

KELLY

Through valleys of sorrow, she walks with grace,

KELLY

Lending strength to those in the hardest race.

KELLY

Her touch, like a gentle breeze in spring,

KELLY

Brings solace to hearts with a broken wing.

KELLY

Oh, Kelly, your name, a symphony rare,

KELLY

A melody that fills the hushed air.

KELLY

In every whisper, in every sigh,

KELLY

Your essence lingers, soaring high.

KELLY

So let us raise a toast to Kelly's name,

KELLY

A beacon of light, a flickering flame.

KELLY

May it shine forever, bright and true,

KELLY

In the hearts of many, both old and new.

KELLY

In the twilight's embrace, Kelly's spirit roams,

KELLY

Amongst the stars, she finds her home.

KELLY

Her laughter echoes through the endless night,

KELLY

A melody of joy, pure and bright.

KELLY

In the quiet moments, when shadows fall,

KELLY

Kelly's presence whispers, answering the call.

KELLY

A gentle reminder of love's sweet refrain,

KELLY

Guiding us through both pleasure and pain.

KELLY

ABOUT THE CREATOR

Walter the Educator is one of the pseudonyms for Walter Anderson. Formally educated in Chemistry, Business, and Education, he is an educator, an author, a diverse entrepreneur, and he is the son of a disabled war veteran. "Walter the Educator" shares his time between educating and creating. He holds interests and owns several creative projects that entertain, enlighten, enhance, and educate, hoping to inspire and motivate you.

Follow, find new works, and stay up to date
with Walter the Educator™
at WaltertheEducator.com

www.ingramcontent.com/pod-product-compliance
Lightning Source LLC
LaVergne TN
LVHW052009060526
838201LV00059B/3941